I0843990

Cover illustration: Armoured troopers pause in a Dutch town, autumn 1944. Uncharacteristically, these men wear the M1941 field jacket rather than the distinctive and preferred jacket of the Armored Force. The 'bocage cutters' welded to the M5 or M5A1 light tank's front were an improvisation borne of necessity in the hedgerow fighting in France. German beach obstacles at Normandy provided the raw material for these ingenious and effective devices, designed by an Ordnance Corps sergeant. The M5 was a 1942 redesign of the earlier M3 tank; by the war's end it had become the standard American light tank.

 UNIFORMS ILLUSTRATED No 14

US ARMY UNIFORMS

EUROPE 1944-1945

CAMERON P. LAUGHLIN &
JOHN P. LANGELLIER

ARMS AND ARMOUR PRESS

Introduction

Published in 1986 by Arms & Armour Press Ltd.,
2–6 Hampstead High Street, London NW3 1QQ.

Distributed in the United States by Sterling
Publishing Co. Inc., 2 Park Avenue, New York,
N.Y.10016.

British Library Cataloguing in Publication Data:
Laughlin, Cameron P.
U.S. Army uniforms: Europe 1944-45.—
(Uniforms illustrated; v. 14)
1. United States, *Army*—Uniforms—History
I. Title   II. Langellier, John P.   III. Series
355.1′4′0973   UC483

ISBN 0-85368-727-7

Editing, design and artwork by Roger Chesneau.
Typesetting by Typesetters (Birmingham) Ltd.
Printed and bound in Italy
by GEA/GEP in association with
Keats European Ltd., London.

*In memory of our fathers, Machinist 2nd Class (CB)
Donald B. Langellier* USNR *and Lieutenant-Colonel
Patrick Laughlin* USMCR, *whose service in the Second
World War fostered our interest in military history.*

◀2
1. (Title spread) Hot chow in the field, January 1945:
men of the 94th Infantry Division come in for rations
delivered by means of a jeep-mounted mobile mess.
Equipped with tyre chains, a 'bustle' rack and a
trailer, such jeeps could carry a disproportionate load
considering their size and weight.
2. With a basic mechanism identical to that of the
M1917A1 machine gun (an important consideration
in saving training time), but air- as opposed to water-
cooled, the .30cal M1919A4 machine gun saw
extensive use throughout the war as a company-level
light weapon. In this role, the gun was mounted on
the M2 tripod, but it also saw widespread use in a
fixed configuration in vehicles. Toting the gun
without its tripod, this trooper carries a Garand rifle
as his personal armament, with full cartridge belt and
an additional fabric bandolier. He has followed a
practice common among American infantrymen, who
would do anything to avoid using the field pack: he
has discarded this encumbrance and is now hand-
carrying a blanket roll loaded with personal gear and
necessities. France, 1944.

The American Army which stormed on to the shores and plummeted
from the skies of the Normandy peninsula in the early hours of 6 June
1944 was, arguably, the most formidable fighting force ever fielded to
that date. While this volume will make no attempt to address its
doctrine, leadership or tactics, it does examine the clothing,
equipment, weapons and vehicles the superlative quality and
overwhelming quantity of which set these men apart from both their
allies and the Axis troops they opposed. This technical capability and
material wealth was the product of the vast industrial capacity of the
United States, coupled with the experiences of two and a half years of
war in North Africa, Sicily, Italy and the Pacific Theatre.

The US Army was in the process of massive change when the attack
on Pearl Harbor brought America into the global conflict. The 1930s
had witnessed vast doctrinal innovation, whilst, in a material sense,
the interwar Army subsisted on still-huge stocks of First World War
surplus. But the new techniques and tactics evidenced in the early
campaigns of the Second World War required substantial new
directions, and the implementation of theories which had already
evolved in the Army's service schools in the decade prior to the
conflict. In one sense, this American response focused on increased
specialization. The War Department saw a need for units which had
never previously existed – ski and mountain troops, special forces,
paratroops, the armoured force – and each new arm developed its own
distinctive garb and equipment in conjunction with the
Quartermaster and Ordnance Corps.

Although Americans devoted considerable ingenuity and effort to
perfecting specialist items for each force, the logistical realities of war
eventually proved this ideal to be unworkable, and by late 1944 the
Army had implemented the opposite policy – the provision of general-
purpose items. The M1943 series of clothing and equipment, first
tested on the Anzio beach-head, was essentially a universal issue,
appropriate for all troops and embodying many of the best qualities of
the specialist items. Its first widespread issue in Europe took place
during the autumn of 1944.

In addition to the two very divergent official approaches to the
Army's needs, the individual soldier inevitably made his own
preferences felt in variety of ways. American fighting men have
traditionally demonstrated little regard for the official stance when it
fails to meet their requirements or tastes. Responding character-
istically, US troops in the Northern European campaign innovated
and invented, adapting to their changing environments and
circumstances, and the lack of adequate preparation for the severe
winter of 1944–45 heightened the incentive for improvisation and
adaptability. From the material viewpoint, this individualistic
approach was an important theme of the campaign – one little noted in
official literature but amply illustrated in the following pages.

Sincere and grateful acknowledgement of assistance provided in the
research and production of this volume should be accorded the
following: the co-operative and competent staff of the Defense Audio
Visual Agency; Charles Cureton, Curator of the Don F. Pratt
Memorial Museum; Lee Ann Brookes; and Wayne Griffin. Particular
thanks are due to Capt. Ray Piluso, Inf., USA, and, of course, to our
wives, Ann and Kit. All the illustrations in this volume are US Army
Official.

Cameron P. Laughlin and John P. Langellier

3. En route to Ireland as part of the initial build-up of American forces in Europe, these US Army troops co-operate with their Navy counterparts in aerial spotting and anti-aircraft gunnery for the convoy. They wear garrison and overseas caps, M1941 jackets and woollen overcoats, as well as inflatable rubber lifebelts. The machine gun is the M1917A1 water-cooled .30cal Browning with improvised butts and tie-downs to prevent tripod skating.

4. Fresh from the United States, 'Yanks' of the 2nd US Infantry Division disembark from their transport in Belfast, Northern Ireland, October 1943. They are dressed in typical combat uniform for the period, are equipped with both M1910/28 field packs and M1936 field bags with full field load, and carry well-stuffed individual barracks bags. Sturdier and more easily transported canvas duffles replaced these last items for transport purposes early in the European campaign. The paper sacks probably contain lunch!

▲3   ▼4

5. In a contrived photograph obviously posed for public consumption back home, an American lieutenant-general provides a black 'medic' with his autograph. The general wears a finely tailored set of Class 'A's with garrison cap, while the aidman wears a mackinaw, the M1 steel helmet, and the special Medical Corps dressing pouches. Extra gear is carried in a kitbag hung by means of a pack suspender snaphook.

6. Training in Armagh, Northern Ireland, these men of the 2nd Infantry Division listen to an address by Lt. Gen. George S. Patton Jr., April 1944. The troops are wearing the herringbone twill OD (olive drab) field uniform; company aidmen employ First World War-vintage Geneva Cross brassards; and the M1936 map case shows to advantage on the staff sergeant's shoulder to the left. The practice of camouflaging helmets with native foliage was not common among US soldiers during this period, although it is a taught soldier-skill today. The 2nd (Indianhead) Division hit the Normandy invasion beaches on D+5 after extensive training in the United Kingdom.

5▲   6▼

▲7

7. Privates serving as part of the Amphibious Landing Force become acquainted with their assault gasmasks and accompanying waterproof carrying bags as they make final preparations for the Normandy invasion, which would begin a few days after this photograph was taken. Fortunately for the Allies, and despite large stocks located near the beaches, the enemy did not use chemical or nerve agents to repel the invaders as they landed. The white arc marking on the helmets was apparently used to designate personnel assigned to amphibious units.

8. Ordnance Corps enlisted women look on as Lt. Iona Sherman demonstrates the use of the 2.5in rocket launcher (variously known as the 'Bazooka' or, early in the war, 'Rocket Gun'). The enlisted WACs wear the standard olive drab wool serge uniform of blouse and trousers, with OD shirt and khaki necktie, while the lieutenant dons the female version of the famous 'pinks and greens' service dress. Arrayed behind the WACs is a full assortment of American small arms of the period, including some non-standard items. Cheltenham, England, 29 May 1944.

▼8

9. The well dressed WAC of 1944 maintained an extensive wardrobe, as is evidenced by this inspection made in Britain at the time. The captain and her sergeant appear in overcoats and exhibit the overseas cap as well as the service cap produced for women. Most female clothing was designed in 1942, but the military's limited experience in providing for the fair sex made several modifications and changes necessary as the war progressed.
10. A 2nd Armored Division 60mm M2 mortar crew work their

piece during manoeuvres in Britain. The smallest mortar in US service, the M2 was based upon the French pattern manufactured by Edgar Brandt; typically, it fired 3lb HE charges at a maximum range of 100yds, and it became the standard light infantry mortar in American service. The troops here all wear the standard-issue winter combat uniform characteristic of the Armored Force, with M1 steel helmets.

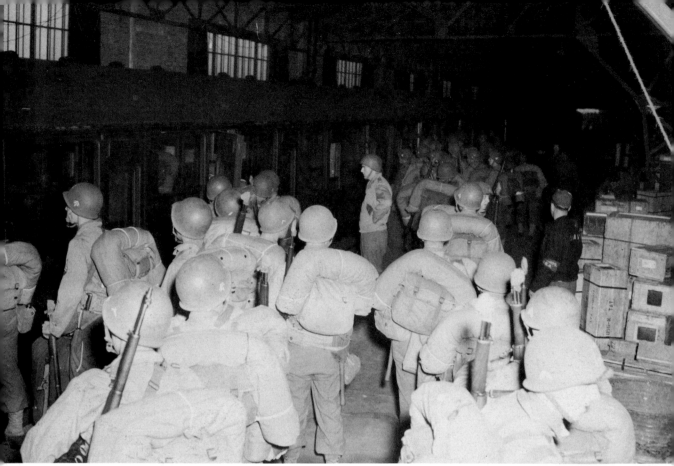

▲11

▼12

11. Having recently arrived at a port in southern England, troops hasten to board a train which will take them to the embarkation points for the invasion of France. Non-commissioned rank is indicated on the sides of the helmets by white-painted designs, a practice uncommon for the time although widespread during the next decade.

12. Assisted by British sailors, American Rangers dismount from a truck on their way to the quayside, Weymouth, Dorset, 1 June 1944; note the censor-obliterated sleeve insignia. Weapons visible include an M1 rifle equipped with a grenade launcher, an M1 carbine, and a 2.5in rocket launcher.

13. Grasping his own copy of General Eisenhower's message to troops before the invasion, a bazookaman of the 101st Airborne Division awaits take-off in the C-47 transport aircraft which will take him to Normandy. He and his comrades are all wearing the distinctive M1941 airborne field uniform and M1C steel helmets; all the helmets bear British-manufactured cotton netting, and some have camouflage strips of burlap 'scrim' woven throughout to further break up their outlines. The reserve chestpacks of the T5-A or T7-A parachutes were more a morale-booster than a practical consideration, since D-Day drops were made at altitudes which would have made their deployment impossible. The 25ft cotton jump ropes enabled troopers to lower themselves if they landed in tree-tops.

14. Ashore! The faces of these assault troops of the 16th Infantry Regiment, 1st Infantry Division, reflect the shock of the early-morning landing and action. Many of the men appear without weapons and equipment (which they probably lost in the surf), several retaining only the M26 USN lifebelts which, soon discarded, littered the invasion beaches.

13▲ 14▼

▲15

15. Moving along the chalk cliffs of Collville-sur-Mer, machine-gunners of the 3rd Battalion, 16th Infantry Regiment, proceed to an inland position. The M1 carbines carried by two of the men were common arms for gunners. The equipment surrounding the casualties at the base of the cliffs consists largely of the ubiquitous life-preserving belts, whilst the ammunition-bearer in the immediate foreground carries well-loaded general-purpose ammunition bags.

16. Movement inland after the invasion beaches had been secured proved both slow and costly. Here an American infantry lieutenant and his radioman sergeant work forward (probably for the photographer) past intermingled bodies of German soldiers and American paratroopers near St.-Lô, July 1944. The two are armed with a .45cal M1911A1 pistol and a .30cal M1 carbine, the two weapons which filled most sidearm roles among American ground forces in the ETO. The M1911A1 was a 1920s modification of the original Browning design, had a seven-round magazine and fired semi-automatically; the M1 carbine, with its lighter calibre and fifteen- (later thirty-) round magazine was intended as a replacement for the pistol in many capacities.

▼16

17. Mortarmen of the 315th Infantry, 79th Division, leave La-Haye-du-Puits, 4 July 1944. Specialized equipment for these troops included the canvas vest for packing mortar rounds, as seen on the man at the rear of the column, and the canvas shoulder pads donned by the three leading troopers, who are taking turns at carrying the tube and baseplate. The netting on the point man's helmet represents an individual whim since it probably came from a vehicle camouflage net.

18. Providing supporting fire with a 60mm mortar in the field in France, these American infantrymen carry a variety of field equipment reflecting old and new issues. Particularly evident are entrenching tools: the soldier at the far left is carrying both an M1910 pick-mattock and an M1910 shovel, while the radioman is carrying the new M1943 entrenching tool from his belt. This last-mentioned item combined the capabilities of a mattock and a shovel in its swivel-mounted head, was more compact than its predecessors, and entirely replaced the M1910 versions when production met demand in the immediate postwar period.

18▼

▲19

▼20

19. Armed and equipped as infantry, these men of a construction battalion of the 9th Air Force await word to begin building an emergency airstrip, somewhere near the landing beaches in France. This photograph was apparently taken in a staging area, since it is doubtful whether the vehicles in the background are integral to the Air Corps unit. The uniforms are typical of the early days of the European campaign: M1941 field jackets; wool or herringbone twill (HBT) trousers; service shoes worn with M1936 canvas leggings; and M1 steel helmet. One wonders what the officer standing at the centre of this group would do with any of his three weapons if the need arose. Note the Engineer Corps branch insignia on his collar.

20. American infantrymen, some marching and others mounted in MB or GPW 'jeeps', move forward on a road in France, July 1944. The quarter-ton vehicles, employed in a wide range of roles, afforded the Allies unprecedented mobility and sped the advance across Europe. In this instance, the jeep-mounted troopers are probably a reconaissance unit.

21. Combat engineers of the 17th Engineer Battalion, 2nd Armored Division, survey a rubble-strewn alley prior to clearing a passage for vehicles, Canisy, France, 27 July 1944. The men use two-piece, camouflaged, herringbone twill summer combat uniforms, newly issued on a limited basis early in the summer of 1944 for Europe but discontinued shortly thereafter allegedly because of combat identification problems with Germans in similar garb. Another difficulty stemmed from the fact that this pattern of camouflage made troops more visible in motion than those wearing standard OD!

22. Another view of the camouflaged combat uniform in service in France, this time near the town of Mont Grocard, 29 July 1944, with an infantry squad. Much of the fighting that summer took place in dense hedgerow country like this; the broken terrain made small unit actions the rule. Even minor gains in ground proved slow and costly.

▲23   ▼24

23. Combat in the bocage. American infantry, lightly equipped for the assault, sprint forward along a hedgerow near Mortain, France, in August 1944. Note that the soldiers have discarded their packs and that each has tucked his jacket, poncho or blanket through his cartridge belt or webbed suspenders.

24. The gun crew of an infantry cannon company man their M3 105mm howitzer, pretentiously dubbed 'Hitler's Doom'. The gunners are from the 2nd Infantry Division, fighting in August 1944 near Brest, France.

25. Just before D-Day, many American GIs received 'skinhead' haircuts as part of combat preparations. The equipment indicates that these men probably belong to the glider-borne component of an airborne division. The artwork on the M1941 field jacket used as the barber's drape is definitely non-regulation (although this type of adornment was fairly common in the ETO), whilst the M1910/18 messkits used as mirrors are most likely a theatrical, rather than a practical, touch. The stainless steel ID tag replaced the old aluminium disc type at the beginning of the war.

26. Rangers wait in transit barges, exhibiting a variety of pre-invasion emotions. The Ranger shoulder sleeve insignia is well in evidence, as are M1 rifles, rubberized assault gasmask bags, a 2.5in rocket launcher and a white pack of Lucky Strike cigarettes, the last a wartime mainstay. Lucky at this point had already 'gone to war' and shed its green pack colouration to free needed pigments for uniform manufacture during the national emergency.

25▲   26▼

27. American Rangers of either the 1st or 5th Battalions (note the painted diamond insignia of the Rangers on the helmet backs) board invasion barges at an English port. They appear in standard infantry uniform and gear, and valuable items such as radios have been fitted with US Navy M26 inflatable lifebelts of their own.

28. Parachute infantrymen provisionally equipped as a ski patrol move out of a village in the French Alps during the winter of 1944. If the original Signal Corps identification of this rare photograph is correct, this temporary conversion of troops from one highly trained military occupation to another is ironic in the extreme. Considerable ingenuity and effort were devoted to the creation of unit-specific gear for both ski and parachute troops at the beginning of the war, and provisional use belies both equipment development and specialized individual training.

29. Partially concealed from observation by camouflage netting, gunners of the 9th Infantry Cannon Company pour out fire at German positions in Brest, summer 1944. They have shed much of their heavy clothing for this hot work with the 105mm M3 howitzer, a field piece designed for 'infantry-artillerymen' early in the war and also supplied to airborne elements. The concept of infantry cannon companies came about in 1941 and went into practice the following year.

30. Serviced by black troops, this 40mm Bofors anti-aircraft gun is representative of one of the most widely used and versatile weapons of the war. Designed in Sweden, and firing a 2lb shell at a rate of 120 rounds per minute with an effective range of 12,000ft, the Bofors was originally intended only for naval use in US service, but changing naval requirements, coupled with the ground forces' demands for more effective anti-aircraft protection, precipitated the dismounting of these guns from vessels and their installation on newly-designed wheeled carriages. With a crew of six and a weight in action of 2.4 tons, the Bofors, which required a prime mover, was installed for the protection of rear areas, bridgeheads and the like.

▲27   ▼28

31. Tank driver Sgt. Joseph Cirillo of the 2nd Armored Division examines one of his vehicle's periscopes prior to moving out, near La Commune, France, 24 July 1944. His typical tanker's combat garb includes the distinctive leather, cloth and composition crash helmet. The sidearm is the M1911A1 automatic pistol, in an M1916 belt holster. The armoured divisions played a crucial role in the breakout from the beach-heads and the subsequent pursuit of the German armies across France.

32. Tankers of the 2nd Armored Division prepare to move out near La Commune, France, in July 1944. The piled Thompson SMGs and M1 carbines constituted standard weaponry for armoured crewmen in the early years of the war, but issues of M3 and M3A1 sub-machine guns augmented these in 1944–45. The tanker on the left has further supplemented 'Uncle Sam's supply with a German P-38 pistol, whilst his comrade at the right carries a privately purchased hunting knife. The tank is an M4 Sherman.

33. Vehicles and men of the 82nd Reconnaissance Battalion, 2nd Armored Division, pass through St. Saver Calvados, August 1944. Artillery fire has rendered the town less than picturesque, and the scout cars proceed with caution through its narrow streets. Recon troops, travelling fast in small units, spearheaded the rapid armoured advance across France and into Germany. Typically, crew members' personal gear covers the outside surfaces of the turrets, bedrolls and M1936 field bags being easily distinguishable.

◀31

32▲   33▼

34. Carefully stepping off the battered ramp of a well-used LCI (Landing Craft, Infantry), the first member of the Forward Communications Zone WAC Detachment lands in France, 5 July 1944. The WACs are wearing the most up-to-date women's version of the M1943 field uniform, although without the accompanying two-buckle field boots. All web equipment and other combat gear is standard (equivalent to the male issue). The shopping bag, clipped by its rope handles to a free pack suspender snapbook, provides a feminine touch to 1st Sgt. Nancy Carter's otherwise GI appearance.

35. Field Marshal Montgomery addresses American officers presented with the Distinguished Service Cross as a result of heroic service in the Normandy invasion. The Americans' clothing represents most of the variations found in combat at the time,

jackets and shirts including (left to right) an M1941 airborne field jacket (worn by Gen. Maxwell Taylor); a winter combat uniform jacket of the Armored Force; two M1933 wool shirts; another 'tanker's jacket; and the ubiquitous M1941 field jacket. The variety of web equipment, including here many items of First World War-vintage, also typified the gear to be seen in the period immediately after 'Overlord'.

36. Here, the camera has captured the women's section of the First Army clothing sales store in full operation, administered by the 581st Quartermaster Sales Co., 6 December 1944. Patrons were primarily WAC officers, Army Nurse Corps (ANC) personnel and Red Cross workers. The recently available M1943 field boot is being tried on in the foreground.

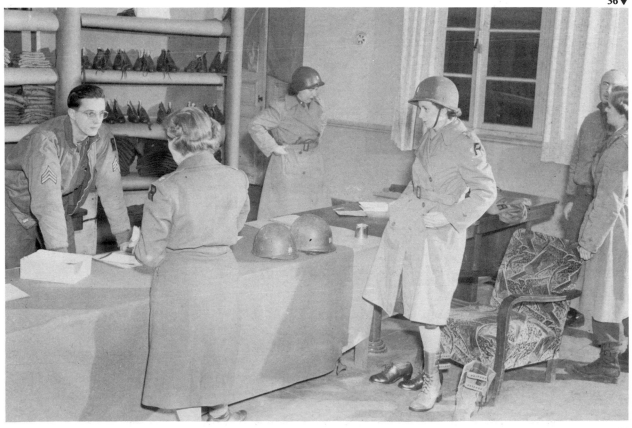

37. Virgil Clifton, an infantry radio sergeant of the 331st Infantry Regiment, stops on a street in Coutances, France, in July 1944. His standard warm-weather combat uniform of olive drab herringbone twill blouse and trousers evolved from cotton HBT work clothing. Clifton's equipment typifies the items issued to an infantryman, with the exception of a captured German leather belt and map case. He has strapped an M3 trench knife to his right leg, and he carries a .45cal M3 sub-machine gun.

38. These nurses of the 10th Field Hospital of the 5th Armored Division were already three-year veterans of service in Egypt and Britain when they posed on a jeep for a Signal Corps photographer at Le Mans, France, in August of 1944. The nurse's non-combatant status is reflected by the wear of Lieutenant's bars (all nurses were officers) on shirt collars, and by the Geneva Cross brassards casually pinned to most blouse sleeves. All but one of the nurses wear the female garb for combat areas which consisted of a herringbone twill blouse and trousers, similar to male issue but developed in 1942 specifically for women and subsequently improved. The variety of footgear reflects the nurses' well-documented loathing for the dismounted-pattern cotton duck leggings.

39. 'His and hers' field wear in the streets of a French town: Tech. Sgt. Clarence Miller points the way to Paris for WAC PFC Lila Hunkins. Lila wears the female version of the M1943 field jacket, while her male companion has donned only the coat-style, OD wool-flannel shirt. The wearing of lipstick and other cosmetics with the field uniform was not uncommon among the WACs of the Second World War.

40. A British MP and two Free French troopers examine a captured German *Soldbuch*, France, August 1944. Clothed and equipped with American matériel, the French are indistinguishable from their US allies, the man on the right wearing the one-piece herringbone twill mechanic's coverall common among armoured crewmen. The vehicle in the background is an M3A1 halftrack (manufactured during the war by International Harvester, White, Autocar and Diamond T), modified with additional compartment armour and featuring camouflage netting and crew members' personal gear stowed on the fenders.

41. Serving beyond the limits of regular operations, reconnaissance troops have typically felt themselves also beyond many of the common restraints of standard military garb and equipment. Against the background of his .30cal M1919A4 machine gun-equipped jeep, 1st Lt. Raymond Yaple of Troop 'C', 4th Cavalry Reconnaissance Squadron, shows some common irregularities. The combination of the olive drab wool shirt and HBT trousers is unusual; the brown knit vest is non-issue, available through the Red Cross or found in parcels from home; and the lieutenant's boots are paratrooper issue (though the wear of these coveted items at this date by a non-jumper was decidedly daring). Yaple is armed with a captured Walther P-38 pistol, and is fuzing TNT blocks; the demolition bag from which the charges have been pulled is one of the least common items of Second World War field equipment.

42. Officers of the 761st Medium Tank Battalion find four-buckle arctics just the thing for heavy mud, along with the M1943 field combat boot. The captains wear the armoured force combat clothing, including the jacket with knitted wool wristlets, collar and waistband and the zipper down the front. The officer on the right protects himself with a trench coat and green knitted wool glove liners.

43. Men of the French First Army victoriously fly their tricolour over recently liberated Belfort, November 1944. Only the Free French helmet insignia and a traditional French military cap on the man at the far left mark their nationality, since these troops received American uniforms and equipment before returning to fight on their home soil.

41 ▶

▼ 42

43 ▶

▲ 44

44. Members of a newly-revived Belgian Regular Army unit pose prior to setting out on a patrol in the American 1st Infantry Division area, September 1944. With the exceptions of the occasional Mauser rifle, and their bizarre means of conveyance, these troops look very much like the American allies who supplied them with both the newly introduced M1943 field uniform and the older M1941 jacket; even their officer is an American lieutenant on loan, and he completes the multinational mixture by carrying a British Mk. II Sten sub-machine gun. These troops were charged with scouting and reconniassance tasks because of their knowledge of the countryside, language and customs.

45. The .30cal US Rifle M1, standardized in 1936 and commonly called the Garand (its inventor's surname), was probably the best infantry rifle employed in any numbers during the Second World War. Its robust design, semi-automatic action and capacity for fine long-range accuracy endeared it to those who, like this American sergeant near Sourbrodt, Germany, depended upon the weapon daily. Although the eight-round magazine capacity was large for its day, the *en bloc* clip from which cartridges fed into the piece proved the Garand's major flaw. The clip, essential for anything other than single shot use, made a distinctive 'clang' as it was ejected when the rifleman fired his last round.

46. The Browning Automatic Rifle (BAR) and M1 rifle, which with the M1 carbine provided basic infantry squad armament, are shown here in action with the 102nd Infantry Division in Germany during February 1945. The cut-down M1905 bayonet (note the 'blood gutter's continuity to the end of the blade), now in M1905E1 configuration, is readily visible, as, at foxhole's rim, are a K-ration supper unit, two M1910/28 haversacks and a pair of grey felt insoles.

▲ 45   ▼ 46

47. The US sub-machine gun M3 was the American answer to the increased use of such weapons on the modern battlefield and to the need for a less expensive alternative to the previously standard Thompson sub-machine gun in its various forms. Inspired by the British Sten and German MP-40, the M3 made extensive use of cheap stampings, and because of an undeniable similarity in outline it was referred to as the 'greasegun'. The M3, and later the M3A1, saw increasing service among troops such as vehicle crewmen and paratroops in 1944–45. Here Pvt. Nathaniel Simmons, assistant driver of an M4 tank, brandishes his 'greasegun' near Nancy, France, November 1944.

48. Carbine and rifle, both designated M1, in a graphic photograph taken during the fighting against German para-troopers in marshlands near St. Germain, France, in July 1944. The men are members of a reconnaissance squadron and wear typically varied garb. The carbine is equipped with a grenade launcher.

47▲   48▼

49. Squad-level automatic fire was provided by the .30cal M1918A2 BAR. An expensive and rugged weapon, the BAR was capable, in its A2 configuration, of both slow and fast full-auto fire, as well as of semi-automatic operation. Because of their weapons' weight (each was slightly more than 19lb), BAR-men were usually physically larger than their comrades. The gunner's basic ammunition load consisted of twelve 20-round box magazines, carried in the M1937 pocketed web belt. Second Infantry Division BAR-man Floyd Rogers, photographed in France in June 1944, sports a German Waffen-SS camouflaged helmet cover (presumably taken from one of his 27 confirmed kills) which fits well over his M1 steel helmet; note, too, that Rogers has sawn half the handle of his M1910 E-tool, rendering it less awkward for belt carriage and for kneeling BAR fire.

50. Redlegs of the 777th Field Artillery Battalion await firing orders near their gun positions in Germany, January 1945. Still a segregated force at the time, the US Army ensured that even aidmen attached to negro units were black. The artilleryman on the left sports an armoured trooper's winter cloth helmet and, surprisingly, holds a Mk. II Sten sub-machine gun rather than an American-made weapon. Note the Geneva Cross brassard pinned to the front of the aidman's pouch.

51. Another man with a preference for unusual weaponry, Pvt. Harry Rogers totes a captured German MP44 (also designated Stg. 44), a fine firearm, made primarily of stampings, and the world's first true assault rifle; his companion, Pvt. Ray Krzyzanowski, cleans his M1 rifle.

◀ **49**

▲52 ▼53

52. Mounted on the M1917A1 tripod, the .30cal watercooled M1917A1 machine gun commanded more terrain and was capable of greater sustained fire than the M1919A4, and was commonly employed as a battalion-level gun. Its sustained-fire capability is indicated here by the continuously linked, fabric-belted ammunition being fed into the gun. The water jacket's evaporative tubing snakes across the foreground of the photograph, and the gunners wear soiled snow-camouflage. Luxembourg, January 1945.

53. A Browning .50cal M2 heavy-barrelled machine gun provides anti-aircraft protection for a Bailey-bridging operation over a German river. The AA-configured M2 was identical to the vehicle- and aircraft-mounted versions, although it was fitted for right-hand charging and with different firing handles. Weighing 82lb and possessing a rate of fire of 450 rounds per minute, the M2 was so versatile that it could be set up for right- or left-hand feed, right- or left-hand charging and manual or electrical firing.

54. Although posing like an accomplished hunter beside a difficult kill, this bazookaman did not inflict all that damage to the big armoured vehicle with his small rocket gun, but the photograph's original caption does indicate that Private Robert Starkey, 16th Infantry Regiment, did his share in knocking out a resultingly difficult-to-identify vehicle. Although the size and penetration of the American 2.5in bazooka round of the Second World War was inadequate for many battlefield tasks, the weapon nonetheless provided the infantryman with anti-tank power he often otherwise lacked, and it proved useful against bunkers as well.

55. At a review following an 82nd Airborne Division medal presentation ceremony, Gens. (left to right) Gavin, Eisenhower, Ridgeway and Brereton illustrate the varieties of service dress uniform common during the latter part of the war. All wear the wool ETO, or 'Ike' jacket, and wool serge trousers, but in varying material and shades common in officers' clothing. Headgear includes the M1C (airborne) steel helmet and liner, the peaked garrison cap, and the wool overseas cap, whilst footwear consists of low-quarter service shoes for the 'leg' officers and the famous jump boot for the airborne types.

54 ▲   55 ▼

33

◀56   57▲   58▼

56. Modelled here by Lt. Gen. Alexander M. Patch, Commander Seventh US Army, the short ETO or 'Ike' jacket was one of the 1943 uniform innovations which received widespread acceptance and use. Inspired by the British battledress blouse, the M1943 wool field jacket (as it was originally called) was intended to be one of the layers worn in winter under the field jacket. It proved inadequate for this task, but because of its natty appearance it was retained by troops as 'walking out dress'. Made famous by General Eisenhower's instant personal adoption of the blouse, the 'Ike' jacket eventually supplanted the long service dress coat in the postwar period.

57. Although beyond the scope of this work, it should be remembered that the Army Air Forces were just that – a portion of the US Army in Europe rather than a separate branch as was later to become the case. Here members of the 356th Fighter Squadron are briefed by the unit's commander before taking off on a mission, at an airstrip near Ober-Olm, Germany. All but two of the pilots wear standard Army wool serge trousers and wool shirts – the two exceptions appear to be garbed in the AN-S-31 summer flying suit – and two of the flyers wear the popular A-2 summer flying jacket. Also evident are a variety of flying helmets, goggles and personal side-arms.

58. Enjoying an historic link-up, particularly the novelty of a Russian female soldier, PFCs of the 69th Infantry Division celebrate at Torgau, Germany. By this date the division's colourful shoulder-sleeve insignia appears to have decorated most of its members' helmets.

59. Pvt. Hershel Brooky surveys the rubble of Cologne, Germany, at the end of the conflict. The famous cathedral's spires rise in the background.
60. Warming up after spending a protracted period in the cold confines of their armoured vehicle, these 2nd Armored Division tankers wear a combination of early- and late-war uniform items. The winter combat overalls and jacket were prescribed before

America's entry into the war, primarily for issue to the Armored Force. Both men have donned M1941 knit caps under their helmets (note the earphone leads on the helmet of the man on the right), while their boots are the very recently issued M1943 type. The censor has obliterated the unit designation on the shoulder sleeve insignia. November 1944.

61–71. The M1 steel helmet and its M1C airborne version replaced the venerable M1917A1 at the beginning of the Second World War. In use in modified forms to the present day, the distinctive American helmet gained symbolic status and saw service in the ETO with a wide variety of coverings and markings.

39

▲72　▼73

72. The wounded driver of a recently knocked-out American 4th Armored Division tank receives treatment from one of his unit's aidmen. The medic wears uniform items, indicating his affiliation with both the Armored Force and the Medical Corps, and these include the winter combat uniform jacket and wool-lined coveralls of the armoured crewman and the marked helmet, along with the Geneva Cross brassard, of the combat aidman – as commonly seen in France. September 1944.

73. Depicting a common expedient among ill-equipped troops in the winter of 1944, this Signal Corps driver wears a field jacket liner and hood fabricated from salvaged GI blankets. Even troops who had received M1943 uniforms improvised blanket-material liners for them, owing to the failure in service of the M1943 wool field ('Ike') jacket.

74. Shortly after the Battle of the Bulge, Pvt. Willard Nipper and Cpl. James Lewis, transport troops with the US 1st Infantry Division in Belgium, spread gravel from the back of a truck to improve traction at a crossroads. Both men try to remain warm in the OD mackinaw with convertible collar (both manners of wearing the garment are shown), at this point an obsolete item but still common among crews of soft-skinned vehicles and other support troops. The corporal's helmet is covered with the closely-woven, US-manufactured helmet net, with elastic retaining band, which first appeared in late 1944; prior to that, US helmet netting issued in the ETO had either been of British origin or had been improvised by the troops themselves.

74▶

▲75 ▼76

75. Breaking down ration and accessory packs in a German farmyard, weary 1st Division service troops provide evidence of some of their supply problems. C-rations, canned fruit, flour, crackers and, appropriately, the 'breakfast of champions' can be discerned amidst the wreckage. February 1945.

76. Advancing in the open across a field, infantrymen of the 10th Armored Infantry, 4th Armored Division, move forward to break through to surrounded airborne troops in Bastogne, 27 December 1944. They fire their M1 rifles as the rest of their comrades stay close to the ground.

77. Members of the 630th Tank Destroyer Battalion who have lost their vehicles in a recent action fight as infantry near Bastogne, Belgium: these veterans are taking cover in shallow rifle pits in a hill position during December 1944. Because much of the campaign in northern Europe proved so mobile, the foxhole served as a defence in this region less frequently than in theatres such as Italy.

78. On the way to the line near Malmedy, Belgium, at the height of the Battle of the Bulge, these American infantry 'non-coms' and privates exhibit an assortment of uniform and equipment items typical of this period in the European campaign. The widespread use of the wool overcoat during the severe winter gave troops a profile not commonly associated with the American infantry. The cloth-topped, four-buckle arctic overshoe, although classed as 'limited standard', afforded protection from cold and wet and helped prevent trenchfoot, a common and debilitating malady during this phase of fighting.

A la population
de
BASTOGNE

▲79 ▼80

◀82

79. Weary, wet and mud-caked, Pvt. Adam Davis and T/5 Milford Sillars of the 110th Infantry Regiment typify the randomly clothed American soldiers of the winter of 1944. The mounting of the pocketed magazine pouch of the M1 carbine on that weapon's buttstock was never intended by its designers but became common practice among troops. Sillars wears the new issue (though it hardly looks it) of the M1943 field jacket and American-made helmet netting with OD elastic retaining band.

80. Armour-supported reconnaissance troops of the 83rd Infantry Division move up to the attack, Bihain, Belgium, 11 January 1945; the tanks are M4 Shermans, in both early and late configurations. Note how the aidman sprinting to the far left stands out even against the white backdrop of the snow because of his brassard and helmet marks. Despite this fact, the Germans claimed that they had difficulty in distinguishing medics, thereby causing a number of these men to be shot by the enemy.

81. The usual preoccupation of American infantry with quality footwear increased with the severity of the European winter. Here, sorting through salvaged footgear and steel helmets, parachute infantrymen of the 101st Airborne Division at Bastogne, Belgium, look for appropriate sizes, 10 January 1945. Boot types represented in the pile include M1941 jump boots, M1943 combat boots, cloth-topped overshoes and service shoes.

82. Airborne troops, both paratroopers and glidermen, demonstrated a fondness for edged weapons and a propensity for modifying gear. Here Private First Class Vernon Haught of the 325th Glider Infantry Regiment of the 82nd Airborne Division returns from outpost duty. He wears the basic M1943 blouse, trousers and combat boots and utilizes an interesting assortment of field equipment. The M1943 trousers have been altered, as was common in airborne units, by the addition of two large leg pockets, patterned after those of the M1941 airborne field trousers. The waistbelt is a captured German item, and supports a privately purchased sheath knife; the knife on Haught's right leg is probably a Mk. III trench knife. Other armament includes an M1 rifle and a 2.5in rocket launcher.

▲83 ▼84

83. The telephone dominated combat communications during the Second World War, with wire tangles such as this marking forward area headquarters and battery positions. Here Cpl. Arthur Marino of Battery 'A', 12th Field Artillery Regiment, 2nd Armored Division, traces a broken line for repair. The Signal Corps CS C-1 tool pouch on the corporal's belt contains pliers and the TL-29 pocket knife necessary for effecting basic field repairs.

84. Shortly after the relief of beseiged Bastogne, a gun crew composed of troops of the 1st Battalion, 327th Glider Infantry Regiment, 101st Airborne Division, service an M9A1 3in gun in a barn near Haguenau. The criss-crossed poles laid upon the tube break up the latter's silhouette.

85. Shortly after the Bulge fighting, men of Company 'E',

23rd Infantry Regiment, 2nd Infantry Division, move up towards Krinkelt, Belgium. They wear the newly issued winter camouflage capes and hoods; the orange circles on the backs of the capes are unit identification devices.

86. Passing the position of an M1919A4 light machine gun and the body of a German soldier as they move to their positions in the Monschau Forest, Germany, in February 1945, men of the 9th Infantry Regiment provide another glimpse of winter camouflage. These troops have further broken up their outlines by winding strips of white fabric around their M1 rifles and carbines – a practice uncommon in the US Army of the period though taught and encouraged today.

▲87 ▼88

87. The effectiveness of the new snow camouflage speaks for itself in this January 1945 photograph of 1st Infantry Division soldiers advancing near Faymonville, Belgium. The men have improvised pack-carrying straps and ropes for bulky blanket rolls, which often substituted for field packs; the outlines of ration cans are seen in the roll of the soldier in left foreground.

88. Field artillerymen serve an M9A1 3in field piece in Belgium at the height of the Ardennes battle. All but two of the crew wear the distinctive winter combat helmet of cotton, lined with wool kersey, which was originally designed for use by the Armored Force.

89. Mortarmen of the 2nd Armored Division fire on enemy strong-points in the outskirts of Amonines, Belgium, in the aftermath of the Ardennes offensive, January 1945. The 81mm mortar is emplaced in the back of an M3 halftrack.

90. After the discovery at Malmedy, Belgium, of massed bodies of American POWs machine-gunned after capture by German SS troops, these black soldiers of the 3200th Quartermaster Service Co. retrieved the corpses from the field. In this photograph, taken shortly thereafter, most types of field outerwear found in the American Army in the European Theatre appear; both the M41 and M43 jackets, the two versions of the OD mackinaw, the officer's overcoat, the enlisted wool overcoat (heavily modified), the field sweater and the tanker's jacket are included, and these are augmented by the woollen knit toque, woollen scarves and the OD wool protective hood. The predominant weapon is the M1 carbine, typical in such units, but notice also the proudly displayed German P-38 pistol.

▲91

91. Members of a graves registration unit perform their tasks on a newly widened road in France early in 1945. The M3A1 halftrack in the foreground is a reconnaissance variant of that vehicle, equipped with one .50cal Browning M2 HB MG and one .30cal Browning MG M1919A4. It has been heavily field-modified, with extended bumper, storage racks (at the rear and on the side) and a left-side access door for the troop compartment.

92. In a very basic form of combined arms operations, infantrymen board tanks to form a fighting team with their armoured comrades as they move through Giessen, Germany, in March 1945. Virtually every type of clothing and equipment issued to field troops in the ETO is visible in this late-war photograph, indicating some of the continuing problems in supplying the fast-moving field force.

93. Mounting men on tanks became increasingly necessary as the Allied armies sped across Europe. Here elements of the 9th Infantry Regiment, 2nd Infantry Division, hitch a ride on winter-camouflaged M4 medium tanks of the 741st Tank Battalion as they head toward Schoneseiffen, Germany, in February 1945. At this late point in the winter these troops are equipped with an improvement over the hooded snow cape – the white field overparka with accompanying overtrousers and improvised helmet covers worn in lieu of the parka's hood.

▼92   93 ►

▲94 ▼95

94. Cigarettes and field dressings: in the lee of a sheltering building, Sgt. Pernell Schillcutt, a company aidman of the 23rd Infantry Regiment, nonchalantly tends the wounds of another 2nd Inf. Div. soldier near Koenigsfeld, Germany. Both men adopt cold/wet-weather gear, the wounded infantryman is well covered by an issue OD rubberized poncho, and the medic wears the much-coveted winter combat trousers. Both soldiers' feet are protected by the four-buckle rubber overshoe, although the infantryman has cut his pair down to just below the level of the gaiter-top of his M1943 combat boots.

95. Engineers of Company 'C', 2nd Combat Engineer Battalion, appear to be completing the job started by retreating Germans in destroying stockpiled Panzerfaust anti-tank weapons, near Bad Neuenahr, Germany, March 1945. These weapons packed more of a punch than the American bazookas.

96. Passing through the ruins of Giessen, Germany, infantrymen of the 9th Regiment ride armoured vehicles of the 741st Tank Battalion in a provisional mounting scheme which saw extensive use in the later days of the war. The Military Policemen in the foreground are of the 2nd Infantry Division, the Harley-Davidson-mounted MP wearing an enormous leather 'kidney belt', a common item among civilian 'bikers' at the time. Motorcycles were gradually supplanted in use by US forces with the ¼-ton MB or GPW jeep.

97. Two common field modifications of the jeep were the 'bustle' rack for carrying personal equipment outside the passenger compartment and the front bumper-mounted wirecutting post (in this case with the spare tyre slid on to it as well). The wirecutter for jeeps was quickly adopted as a counter to the simple but effective German practice of stringing barely visible cables across roadways as obstacles in the path of the Allied advance. The Medical Corps jeep upon which the cutter is mounted is clearly marked as to function, and is equipped for transporting litter-borne patients. Other vehicles clustered here in a street in Miesenheim, Germany, in March 1945 include M3A1 halftracks and M4 tanks, all from the 11th Armored Division.

◀98   99▲

98. Medics in action near Trier, Germany, in March 1945 aid a 10th Armored Division engineer who has survived a mine detonation. Rubble from the explosion litters the ground, intermingled with an expended morphine syringe and discarded packaging from numerous Carlisle field dressings. Aidmen have stencilled their service numbers on the crowns of their helmets.

99. Warily watching for enemy movement on the Rhine bridge at Bonn, Germany, these 1st Infantry Division men have positioned themselves near the wreckage of a German tank; note the fragments of armour plating and the hatch blown from the vehicle, on the ground in the centre of the photograph. The soldier on the right wears the M1941 field jacket, with an attached hood from an M1943 field jacket – an unusual but sensible improvisation.

100. Pinned down near Scharitz, Austria, men of the 103rd Infantry Division help their wounded captain out of the line of fire and seek cover in a depression near a fence line. Note the heavily sandbagged M4 tank on the road.

100▼

▲101 ▼102

101. Riflemen of the 1st Infantry Division pause behind cover as combat engineers remove a German roadblock under fire, April 1945. At this late date, these men still utilize the M1936 field jacket, yet to be replaced by the new pattern of 1943. M1936 wirecutters in their cotton duck pouch of the same model hang from the corporal's belt; this compact and useful soldier's tool remained an item of issue well into the 1970s.

102. 79th Infantry Division troops engaged in wiring rifle grenades for demolitions work (probably minefield clearing) in Germany, February 1945. The warrant officer, junior grade, on the right wears insignia indicating his uncommon rank on both his field jacket and steel helmet, but wartime censoring has partially obscured his division's Cross of Lorraine shoulder patch. The assault gas-mask bag notably contains something other than a protective mask; it was common soldier practice in the ETO to discard this seemingly redundant piece of equipment and use the empty bag as a haversack.

103. Trailed by a fellow combat engineer equipped with a metal-tipped mine-probe, and casually observed by other 1st Infantry Division troops, Pvt. Mike Redmond checks road shoulders with a mine detector near a German barricade in Blesheim, Germany, March 1945. The parked CCKW 2½-ton truck in the background bears an ETO ringed-star ('invasion') device on its bonnet.

104. Division or corps heavy artillery perform a firing mission in Germany, 1945. The purpose-designed 155mm gun, mounted on the M4 chassis (with shared M4 characteristics) and designated M40, was common in the ETO in this role; also typical is the battery's well entrenched emplacement.

105. Preparing to retake Magdeburg after encountering their strongest resistance since the Rhine crossing, the 2nd Armored Division forces re-form on the city's outskirts. Well in evidence in this photograph are a very heavily burdened MB or GPW jeep, a menacing-looking M10 tank destroyer, a 2.5in rocket launcher with accompanying ammunition bag, and the ubiquitous Garand rifle.

106. Intending to provide Hitler with some special eggs from their field piece, at a position near Lauterback, Germany, in March 1945, these two gunners wear a variety of new and old issues. The soldier to the right has equipped himself with a knife made from a Collins machete, sheathed in an M8 scabbard.

107. An American infantryman draws a bead with his M1 Garand during street fighting in Germany. His bulging pockets and slung blanket roll indicate that he has discarded his field pack, carrying his remaining gear on his cartridge belt. The equipment includes a bayonet, a fragmentation grenade, an E-tool and an OD cotton bandolier of ammunition to supplement that found in the cartridge belt.

108. En route to a footbridge crossing of the Roer River, First US Army soldiers halt in the streets of Kufferath, Germany, in February 1945. Hostile artillery continues to present a threat, but communications wires already festoon the town's damaged buildings.

109. Tank destroyers in a battery firing position near the Roer River, December 1944. Evolving from the M4 tank, the M10 3in Gun Motor Carriage (GMC) was purpose-built as an effective counter to typically superior German armour. The M36 was a later development, first appearing with units in 1942; it boasted a long-barrelled 90mm gun, adapted (like the infamous German '88') from a contemporary anti-aircraft piece. This unit is well emplaced and is apparently ready to support the river crossing.

109 ▼

248431

▲110

110. 'Dogface': the American infantryman as he appeared near the end of the war. Pvt. Gerald Cotton of the 1st Infantry Division awaits orders before crossing the Roer River at Schneidhausen, Germany, in February 1945 with cotton packs, spare bandoliers of ammunition crossed over the chest and extra grenades for the assault. He retains the USN M26 life-preserving belt, used on most beach and river assaults in the ETO, and hauls additional gear in a burlap sandbag clamped under his left arm. He secures his grenades with twine. The bayonet is either an M1905E1 or an M1 – both standard for the M1 rifle – carried in the M7 scabbard.

111. The DD (Duplex Drive) 'swimming' tanks which fared so badly in the surf off the Normandy invasion beaches proved useful for crossing the more placid rivers of Germany. The DDs were

M4A3 Sherman tanks but were propeller-driven when waterborne via a power take-off arrangement; the collapsible canvas screens, stiffened with steel tubing and pneumatically raised, provided bouyancy. The DD seen here is evidently sitting on a submerged portion of the river bank, since it is not riding as low in the water as would a fully immersed tank. In the foreground an improvised river craft, a motor-equipped bridging pontoon, appears; in the background 'alligators' ferry Seventh Army infantrymen to the opposite shore. Germany, March 1945.

112. River assault in Germany. With troops already deployed on the opposite bank, infantrymen of the 'Big Red One's 16th Regiment cross the Weser River, striking Furstenberg from Wehrden, Germany, April 1945.

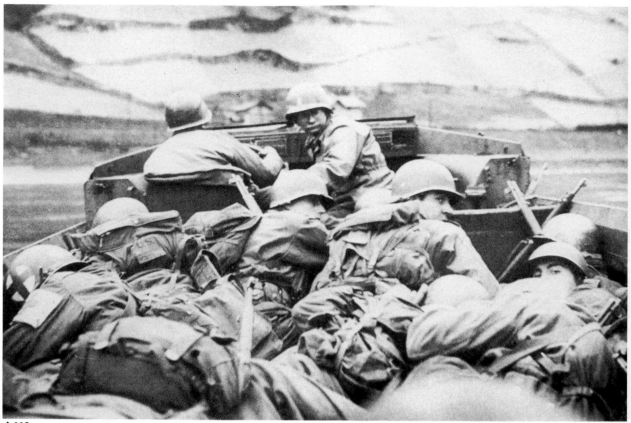

▲113

▼114

113. Another view of a river assault. These men, some of whom seem incredulous of the risks the photographer is taking, are completely equipped and uniformed with the latest generation of gear. Particularly evident are well-stocked field combat packs.

114. Ashore on the enemy-held side of a German river, infantrymen leave the tenuous shelter of their amphibious DUKWs for cover on land. One of the most successful vehicles of the war – 21,000 were built by the end of the conflict – the aptly named DUKW was nearly 30ft long and weighed seven tons. It could carry thirty-five men on land and approximately fifty afloat, and was driven in this latter mode by a rear-mounted propeller.

115. Shoot anything that moves in the water! Justly wary of German underwater demolition teams, American commanders posted marksmen to guard river crossings, pontoons and bridges.

116. Reflecting the American tanker's wariness as a result of armour-versus-armour duels with more heavily armed and better-protected German vehicles, these M4 tanks of the seasoned 2nd Armored Division have been provided with layers of sandbags, encased in wire mesh (note the cleared area around the leading tank's coaxial machine gun). A less common practice which accomplished the same end was the application of layers of cement to the exterior surfaces of tanks. Observed by a surprising number of military service-aged German male civilians, these Ninth Army tanks are rolling through Ahlen, April 1945.

115▲

116▼

▲117 ▼118

117. Striding through the ruins of Cologne, Germany, three members of the 325th Glider Infantry Regiment of the 82nd Airborne Division enjoy what is left of the town's attractions. Clothed completely in late-war issue, their appearance presents little in common with their comrades of earlier campaigns.

118. Three company commanders of the Big Red One's 18th Infantry Regiment demonstrate some non-standard uniform items, February 1945. Each is a veteran of the Division's campaigns in North Africa, Sicily and on the continent since they proudly wear insignia indicating that service. The combat infantryman's badge (above left breast pockets) and gold-embroidered 'Hershey Bars' (each indicating six months of overseas service) were never intended to be worn on the field jacket: the correct usage is illustrated by the captain in the centre, wearing the M1943 ETO jacket. He has also secured the much-prized high-top shoepac – never available in sufficient quantities in Europe.

119. In a much-publicized link-up, Maj. Gen. Clarence Huebner of the US V Corps meets with Maj. Gen. Backenof of the Russian 34th Corps on the banks of the Elbe River, April 1945. Huebner and the accompanying 2nd Infantry Division captain both wear a combination of Class 'A' and combat gear for this ceremonial meeting. The use of the green cloth combat leader's tab on the general's shoulder straps was not condoned for officers of this rank.

120. Army Nurse Bonita Berkshire and her groom, Lt. Col. John H. Himelick, enjoy an unusual wedding conveyance – field litters carried by German prisoners of war. The newlyweds both wear their respective versions of the service dress as it had developed by the end of the war, whilst the colonel sports privately purchased dress shoes, worn in conjunction with the salmon trousers and olive green coat which made up the well-known 'pinks and greens' uniform.

▲121

121. Private Ruth Jones' trench coat was classified a 'limited standard' item when this picture was taken in England during May 1945. A belt and a hood formed part of the coat, as did a button-in lining for foul weather. The men around her display both M1943 field jackets and the wool 'Ike' jacket, and all save the man standing to the left of the young boy wear overseas caps.

122. Wearing the curious combination of Class 'A' and battle gear which predominated during this period, SHAEF (Supreme Headquarters Allied Expeditionary Forces) troops pass in review before General of the Army Dwight D. Eisenhower. Service dress blouses and trousers are worn in conjunction with M1 steel helmets, M1943 combat boots and webbed equipment appropriate to the weapons carried. The officers in the background are British recipients of the American Distinguished Service Cross.

▼122